120 GREAT IMPRESSIONIST PAINTINGS

CD-ROM and Book

Edited by
Carol Belanger Grafton

Dover Publications, Inc.
Mineola, New York

The CD-ROM in this book contains all of the images. Each image has been saved in 300-dpi high-resolution and 72-dpi Internet-ready JPEG formats. There is no installation necessary. Just insert the CD into your computer and call the images into your favorite software (refer to the documentation with your software for further instructions).

Within the Images folder on the CD, you will find two additional folders—"High Resolution JPG" and "JPG." Every image has a unique file name in the following format: xxx.JPG. The first 3 digits of the file name correspond to the number printed under the image in the book. The last 3 letters of the file name, "JPG," refer to the file format. So, 001.JPG would be the first file in the folder.

Also included on the CD-ROM is Dover Design Manager, a simple graphics editing program for Windows that will allow you to view, print, crop, and rotate the images.

For technical support, contact:
Telephone: 1 (617) 249-0245
Fax: 1 (617) 249-0245
Email: dover@artimaging.com
Internet: **http://www.dovertechsupport.com**
The fastest way to receive technical support is via email or the Internet.

Copyright

Copyright © 2007 by Dover Publications, Inc.
Electronic images copyright © 2007 by Dover Publications, Inc.
All rights reserved.

Bibliographical Note

120 Great Impressionist Paintings CD-ROM and Book, is a new work, first published by Dover Publications, Inc., in 2007.

Dover Electronic Clip Art®

International Standard Book Number: 0-486-99774-X

Manufactured in the United States of America
Dover Publications, Inc., 31 East 2nd Street, Mineola, N.Y. 11501

002. ALBERT BAERTSOEN
Ghent, Evening; 1903

001. HARRIET BACKER
Blue Interior; 1883

004. FRÉDÉRIC BAZILLE
View of the Village; 1868

003. FRÉDÉRIC BAZILLE
Summer Scene; 1869

006. FRANK BENSON
The Black Hat; 1904

005. FRÉDÉRIC BAZILLE
Study of Flowers; 1866

008. FRANK BENSON
The Sisters; 1889

007. FRANK BENSON
Sunlight; 1909

010. Jacques-Emile Blanche
Jeune fille rêveuse, portrait de Berthi Capel; 1897

009. Jean Béraud
Waiting, Paris, Rue de Chateaubriand; 1900

011. Pierre Bonnard
The Letter; 1906

012. Pierre Bonnard
Dining Room in the Country; 1913

013. MARIE BRACQUEMOND
On the Terrace at Sèvres; 1880

014. JOHN LESLIE BRECK
Garden at Giverny; 1890

015. GUSTAVE CAILLEBOTTE
Paris, the Place de l'Europe on a Rainy Day; 1877

016. GUSTAVE CAILLEBOTTE
Le pont de l'Europe; 1877

017. GUSTAVE CAILLEBOTTE
The Bridge at Argenteuil and the Seine; 1885

018. MARY CASSATT
The Garden; 1880

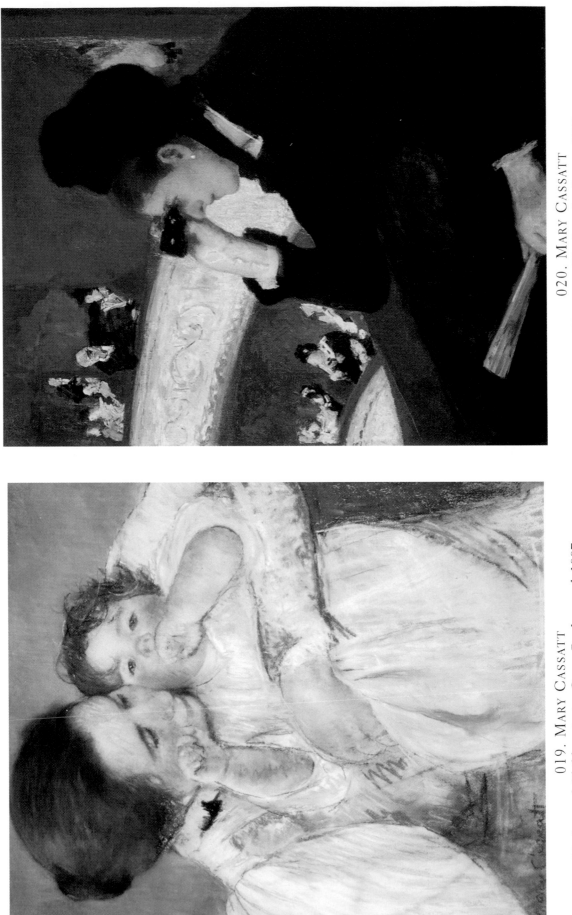

020. MARY CASSATT
Woman in Black at the Opera; 1879

019. MARY CASSATT
Mother and Child against a Green Background; 1887

022. PAUL CÉZANNE
Woman in Blue; 1900

021. MARY CASSATT
The Cup of Tea; 1880

023. PAUL CÉZANNE
Still Life with a Ginger Jar and Eggplants; 1893–94

024. PAUL CÉZANNE
Bathers; 1890–92

025. PAUL CÉZANNE
Monte Sainte-Victoire above the Tholonet Road; 1896–98

026. PAUL CÉZANNE
The Cardplayers; 1892–95

027. WILLIAM CHADWICK
On the Porch; 1908

028. WILLIAM MERRITT CHASE
End of Season; 1885

029. WILLIAM MERRITT CHASE
A Friendly Call; 1895

030. COLIN CAMPBELL COOPER
Cottage Interior; n.d.

031. PAUL CORNOYER
Rainy Day, Madison Square, New York; 1907–08

032. EDGAR DEGAS
The Millinery Shop; 1882

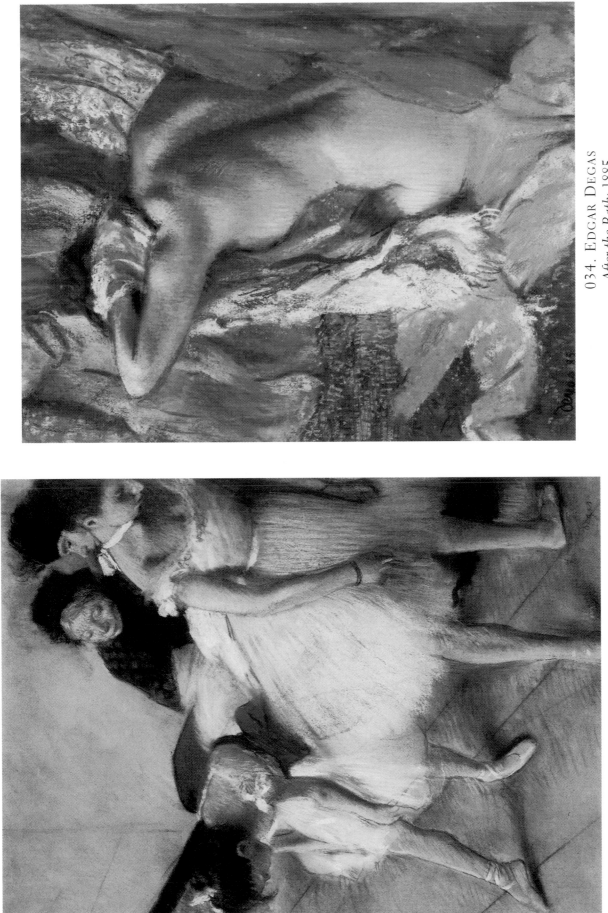

034. EDGAR DEGAS
After the Bath; 1885

033. EDGAR DEGAS
Before the Rehearsal; 1880

036. EDGAR DEGAS
Café-Concert at the 'Ambassadeurs'; 1876

035. EDGAR DEGAS
L'Absinthe; 1876

037. Edgar Degas
The Race Track; Amateur Jockeys near a Carriage; 1877–80

038. Jean-Louis Forain
Woman Smelling Flowers; 1883

039. PAUL GAUGUIN
Café at Arles; 1888

040. PAUL GAUGUIN
Tahitian Landscape; 1891

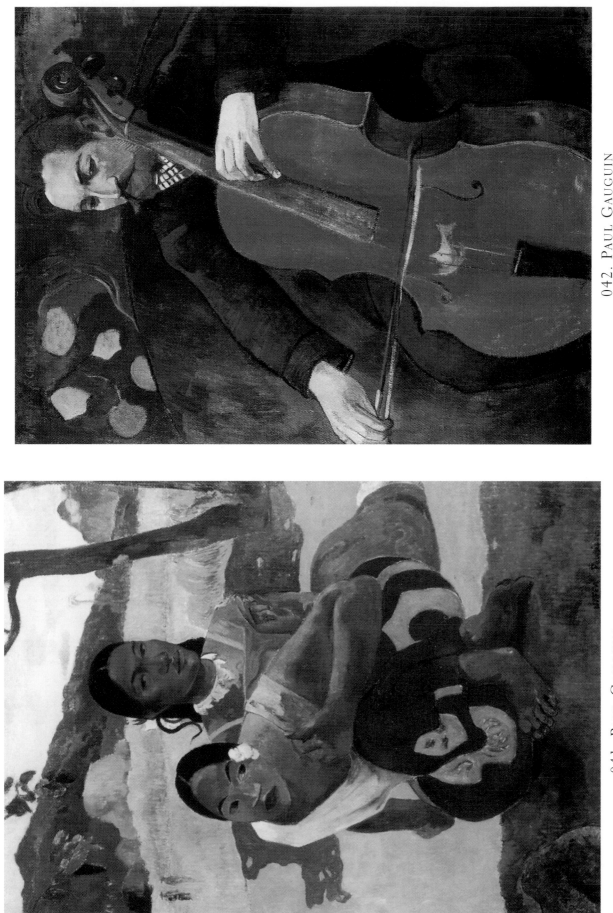

042. PAUL GAUGUIN
Upaupa Schneklud; 1894

041. PAUL GAUGUIN
When will you marry?; 1892

044. WILLIAM GLACKENS
Mahone Bay; 1911

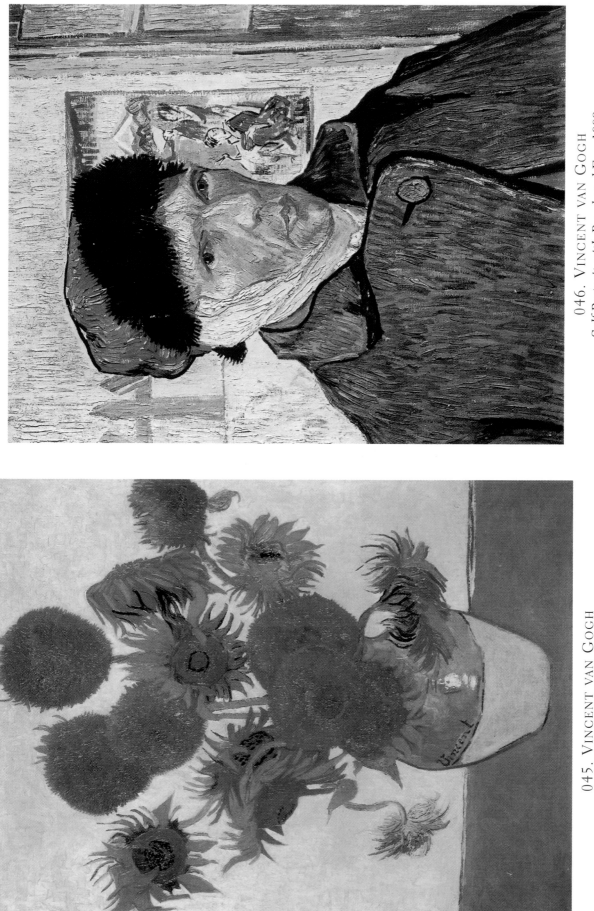

046. VINCENT VAN GOGH
Self-Portrait with Bandaged Ear; 1889

045. VINCENT VAN GOGH
Sunflowers; 1888

047. VINCENT VAN GOGH
Starry Night; 1889

048. VINCENT VAN GOGH
Van Gogh's Bedroom; 1888

050. EVA GONZALES
Morning Awakening; 1877–78

051. Jean-Baptiste Armand Guillaumin
Quai de la Gare, Snow; 1875

052. Philip Leslie Hale
The Crimson Rambler; 1908

054. CHILDE HASSAM
Fifth Avenue at Washington Square; 1891

053. CHILDE HASSAM
Allies Day, May, 1917

056. CHILDE HASSAM
Rue Montmartre; 1889

055. CHILDE HASSAM
The Room of Flowers; 1894

057. ROBERT HENRI
Girl Seated by the Sea; 1893

058. ERNEST LAWSON
Spring Night, Harlem River; 1913

060. EDOUARD MANET
Peonies; 1864

059. MAXIMILIEN LUCE
Notre Dame; 1899

061. EDOUARD MANET
Boating; 1874

062. EDOUARD MANET
A Bar at the Folies-Bergère; 1881–82

064. EDOUARD MANET
Jeanne: Spring; 1881

063. EDOUARD MANET
The Plum; 1878

065. EDOUARD MANET
Steamboat, Seascape or *Sea View, Calm Weather;* 1864–65

066. ALFRED MAURER
An Arrangement; 1901

067. Willard Leroy Metcalf
Gloucester Harbor; 1895

068. Richard Miller
The Toilette; 1914

070. CLAUDE MONET
Rouen Cathedral, Portal and Tour d'Albane, Full Sunlight, Harmony in Blue and Gold; 1894

069. CLAUDE MONET
Waterlilies; 1914

072. CLAUDE MONET
The Walk, Lady with a Parasol; 1875

071. CLAUDE MONET
The Artist's Garden at Vétheuil; 1880

073. CLAUDE MONET
The Highway Bridge at Argenteuil; 1874

074. CLAUDE MONET
Terrace at Sainte-Adresse; 1867

075. CLAUDE MONET
Houses of Parliament, London, Sun Breaking through the Fog; 1904

076. BERTHE MORISOT
Summer's Day; 1879

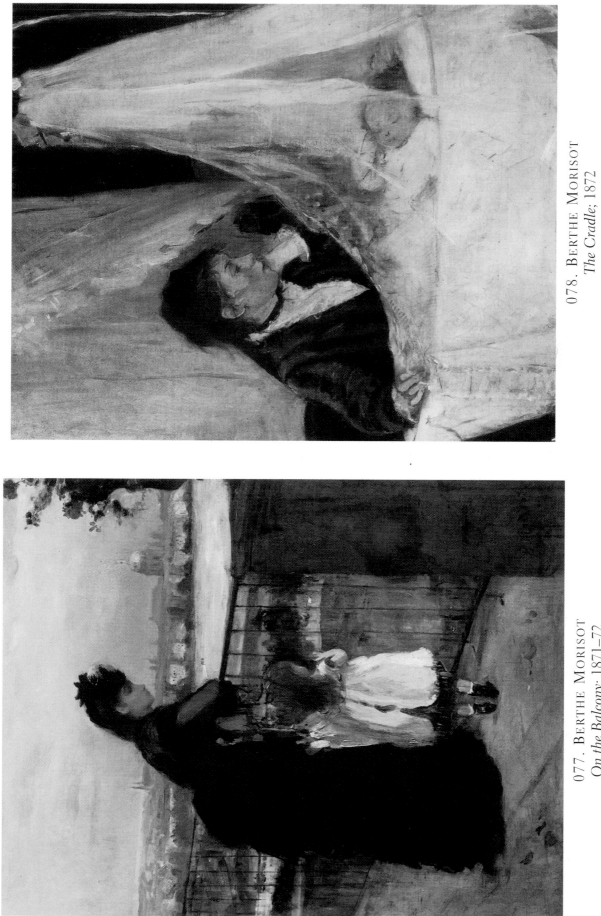

078. Berthe Morisot
The Cradle; 1872

077. Berthe Morisot
On the Balcony; 1871–72

079. Berthe Morisot
At the Ball; 1875

080. Camille Pissarro
Place du Théâtre Français, Rain; 1898

081. CAMILLE PISSARRO
The Shepherdess; 1881

082. CAMILLE PISSARRO
The Garden of Les Mathurins at Pontoise; 1876

083. CAMILLE PISSARRO
The Red Roofs, Corner of a Village, Winter; 1887

084. JEAN-FRANÇOIS RAFFAELLI
Boulevard in Paris; 1888

085. EDWARD REDFIELD
Lower New York; 1910

086. ROBERT REID
Woman with a Vase of Irises; 1906

087. PIERRE-AUGUSTE RENOIR
The Luncheon of the Boating Party; 1881

088. PIERRE-AUGUSTE RENOIR
Oarsmen at Chatou; 1879

090. PIERRE-AUGUSTE RENOIR
La Loge; 1874

089. PIERRE-AUGUSTE RENOIR
Vase of Flowers; 1886

092. THEODORE ROBINSON
The Wedding March; 1892

093. THEODORE ROBINSON
Chicago Columbian Exposition; 1894

094. GUY ROSE
The Green Parasol; 1909

096. JOHN SINGER SARGENT
Paul Helleu Sketching with his Wife; 1889

098. GEORGES-PIERRE SEURAT
A Sunday Afternoon on the Island of La Grand Jatte; 1884–86

099. GEORGES-PIERRE SEURAT
Bathing at Asnières; 1883

100. PAUL SIGNAC
Boulevard de Clichy, Snow; 1886

101. Alfred Sisley
The Bridge at Villeneuve-la-Garenne; 1872

102. Alfred Sisley
The Flood at Port-Marly; 1876

104. ROBERT SPENCER
Repairing the Bridge; 1913

106. PHILIP WILSON STEER
Summer at Cowes; 1888

107. EDMUND CHARLES TARBELL
Three Sisters—A Study in June Sunlight; 1890

108. EDMUND CHARLES TARBELL
The Breakfast Room; 1903

110. HENRI DE TOULOUSE-LAUTREC
Woman with Gloves (Honorine Platzer); 1891

109. JAN TOOROP
Three Women with Flowers; 1885–86

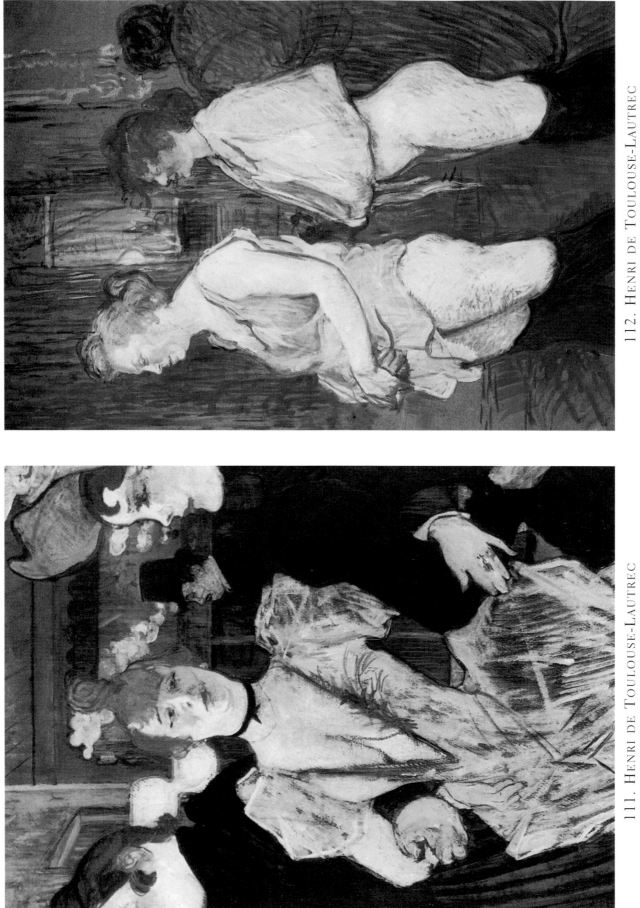

112. HENRI DE TOULOUSE-LAUTREC
Rue des Moulins: The Medical Inspection; 1894

111. HENRI DE TOULOUSE-LAUTREC
La Goulue Arriving at the Moulin Rouge with Two Women; 1892

113. HENRI DE TOULOUSE-LAUTREC
Ball at the Moulin Rouge; 1889–90

114. HENRI DE TOULOUSE-LAUTREC
The Toilette; 1889

116. ROBERT VONNOH
In Flanders Field—Where Soldiers Sleep and Poppies Grow; 1890

117. EDOUARD VUILLARD
Child in a Room; 1900

118. J. ALDEN WEIR
Against the Window; 1884

119. J. Alden Weir
Willimantic, Connecticut; 1903

120. Theodore Wendel
Bridge at Ipswich; 1905

List of Works

001. Harriet Backer [1845–1932] ; *Blue Interior;* 1883; oil on canvas; 33⅛" x 26" (84 x 66 cm).

002. Albert Baertsoen [1866 –1922]; *Ghent, Evening;* 1903; oil on canvas; 61" x 59⅜" (155 x 151 cm).

003. Frédéric Bazille [1841–70]; *Summer Scene;* 1869; oil on canvas; 51⅛" x 35" (130 x 89 cm).

004. Frédéric Bazille [1841–70]; *View of the Village;* 1868; oil on canvas; 20" x 13¾" (51 x 35 cm).

005. Frédéric Bazille [1841–70]; *Study of Flowers;* 1866; oil on canvas; 38¼" x 34⅝" (97 x 88 cm).

006. Frank Benson [1862–1951]; *The Black Hat;* 1904; oil on canvas; 40¼" x 32" (101.6 x 81.3 cm).

007. Frank Benson [1862–1951]; *Sunlight;* 1909; oil on canvas; 32¼" x 20" (81.9 x 50.8 cm).

008. Frank Benson [1862–1951]; *The Sisters;* 1889; oil on canvas; 40" x 39½" (101.6 x 100.3 cm).

009. Jean Béraud [1849–1935]; *Waiting, Paris, Rue de Chateaubriand;* 1900; oil on canvas; 22" x 15½" (56 x 39.5 cm).

010. Jacques-Emile Blanche [1861–1942]; *Jeune fille rêveuse, portrait de Berthi Capel;* 1897; oil on canvas; 35" x 28¾" (89 x 73 cm).

011. Pierre Bonnard [1867–1947]; *The Letter;* 1906; oil on canvas; 21⅝" x 18¾" (55 x 47.5 cm).

012. Pierre Bonnard [1867–1947]; *Dining Room in the Country;* 1913; oil on canvas; 64¾" x 81" (164.5 x 205.7 cm).

013. Marie Bracquemond [1840–1916]; *On the Terrace at Sèvres;* 1880; oil on canvas; 34⅝" x 45¼" (87.9 x 114.9 cm).

014. John Leslie Breck [1860–99]; *Garden at Giverny;* 1890; oil on canvas; 18" x 21⅞" (45.7 x 55.5 cm).

015. Gustave Caillebotte [1848–94]; *Paris, the Place de l'Europe on a Rainy Day;* 1877; oil on canvas; 83½" x 108¾" (212.2 x 276.2 cm).

016. Gustave Caillebotte [1848–94]; *Le pont de l'Europe;* 1877; oil on canvas; 41⅜" x 51⅛" (105 x 130 cm).

017. Gustave Caillebotte [1848–94]; *The Bridge at Argenteuil and the Seine;* 1885; oil on canvas; 25½" x 32¼" (65 x 82 cm).

018. Mary Cassatt [1844–1926]; *The Garden;* 1880; oil on canvas; 26" x 37" (66 x 94 cm).

019. Mary Cassatt [1844–1926]; *Mother and Child against a Green Background;* 1887; pastel; 21⅝" x 17¾" (55 x 45 cm).

020. Mary Cassatt [1844–1926]; *Woman in Black at the Opera;* 1879; oil on canvas; 31½" x 25½" (80 x 64.8 cm).

021. Mary Cassatt [1844–1926]; *The Cup of Tea;* 1880; oil on canvas; 36⅜" x 26" (54.3 x 66 cm).

022. Paul Cézanne [1839–1906]; *Woman in Blue;* 1900; oil on canvas; 34⅝" x 28" (87.9 x 71.1 cm).

023. Paul Cézanne [1839–1906]; *Still Life with a Ginger Jar and Eggplants;* 1893–94; oil on canvas; 28½" x 36¼" (72.4 x 92 cm).

024. Paul Cézanne [1839–1906]; *Bathers;* 1890–92; oil on canvas; 21⅜" x 26" (54.3 x 66 cm).

025. Paul Cézanne [1839–1906]; *Monte Sainte-Victoire above the Tholonet Road;* 1896–98; oil on canvas; 30¾" x 39" (78 x 99 cm).

026. Paul Cézanne [1839–1906]; *The Cardplayers;* 1892–95; oil on canvas; 17¾" x 22½" (45 x 57 cm).

027. William Chadwick [1879–1962]; *On the Porch;* 1908; oil on canvas; 24" x 30" (61 x 76.2 cm).

028. William Merritt Chase [1849–1916]; *End of Season;* 1885; pastel on paper; 13" x 17¾" (33 x 45 cm).

029. William Merritt Chase [1849–1916]; *A Friendly Call;* 1895; oil on canvas; 30⅛" x 48¼" (76.5 x 12.5 cm).

030. Colin Campbell Cooper [1856–1937]; *Cottage Interior;* n.d.; oil on canvas; 20" x 24" (50.8 x 61 cm).

031. Paul Cornoyer [1864–1923]; *Rainy Day, Madison Square, New York;* 1907–08; oil on canvas; 22¼" x 27¼" (56.5 x 69.2 cm).

032. Edgar Degas [1834–1917]; *The Millinery Shop;* 1882; oil on canvas; 39¼" x 43⅜" (100 x 110 cm).

033. Edgar Degas [1834–1917]; *Before the Rehearsal;* 1880; pastel on paper; 24¾" x 18⅞" (62.9 x 47.9 cm).

034. Edgar Degas [1834–1917]; *After the Bath;* 1885; pastel on paper; 25⅛" x 19⅝" (63.8 x 49.2 cm).

035. Edgar Degas [1834–1917]; *L'Absinthe;* 1876; oil on canvas; 36¼" x 26¾" (92.1 x 67.9 cm).

036. Edgar Degas [1834–1917]; *Café-Concert at the 'Ambassadeurs';* 1876; pastel over monotype; 14½" x 10⅝" (37 x 27 cm).

037. Edgar Degas [1834–1917]; *The Race Track; Amateur Jockeys near a Carriage;* 1877–80; oil on canvas; 26" x 32" (66 x 81 cm).

038. Jean-Louis Forain [1852–1931]; *Woman Smelling Flowers;* 1883; pastel on paper; 35" x 31" (88.9 x 78.7 cm).

039. Paul Gauguin [1848–1903]; *Café at Arles;* 1888; oil on canvas; 28⅜" x 36¼" (72 x 92 cm).

040. Paul Gauguin [1848–1903]; *Tahitian Landscape;* 1891; oil on canvas; 26¾" x 36⅜" (67.9 x 92.4 cm).

041. Paul Gauguin [1848–1903]; *When will you marry?;* 1892; oil on canvas; 40" x 30½" (101.5 x 77.5 cm).

042. Paul Gauguin [1848–1903]; *Upaupa Schneklud;* 1894; oil on canvas; 36½" x 28⅞" (92.5 x 73.5 cm).

043. William Glackens [1870–1938]; *Chez Mouquin;* 1905; oil on canvas; 48" x 39" (121.9 x 99.1 cm).

044. William Glackens [1870–1938]; *Mahone Bay;* 1911; oil on canvas; 26⅛" x 31¼" (66.4 x 79.4 cm).

045. Vincent van Gogh [1853–90]; *Sunflowers;* 1888; oil on canvas; 32" x 25¾" (42.5 x 31.5 cm).

046. Vincent van Gogh [1853–90]; *Self-Portrait with Bandaged Ear;* oil on canvas; 1889; 23⅝" x 19¼" (60 x 49 cm).

047. Vincent van Gogh [1853–90]; *Starry Night;* 1889; oil on canvas; 29" x 36¼"(73.7 x 92.1 cm).

048. Vincent van Gogh [1853–90]; *Van Gogh's Bedroom;* 1888; oil on canvas; 28⅜" x 35⅜" (72 x 90 cm).

049. Vincent van Gogh [1853–90]; *Portrait of Doctor Gachet;* 1890; oil on canvas; 26⅜" x 22" (67 x 56 cm).

050. Eva Gonzales [1849–83]; *Morning Awakening;* 1877–78; oil on canvas; 32" x 39⅜" (81.3 x 100 cm).

051. Jean-Baptiste Armand Guillaumin [1841–1927]; *Quai de la Gare, Snow;* 1875; oil on canvas; 20" x 24" (50.5 x 61.2 cm).

052. Philip Leslie Hale [1865–1931]; *The Crimson Rambler;* 1908; oil on canvas; 25" x 30" (63.5 x 76.2 cm).

053. Childe Hassam [1859–1935]; *Allies Day, May, 1917;* oil on canvas; 36⅞" x 30⅜" (93.5 x 77 cm).

054. Childe Hassam [1859–1935]; *Fifth Avenue at Washington Square;* 1891; oil on canvas; 22" x 16" (56 x 40.6 cm).

055. Childe Hassam [1859–1935]; *The Room of Flowers;* 1894; oil on canvas; 34" x 34" (86.4 x 86.4 cm).

056. Childe Hassam [1859–1935]; *Rue Montmartre;* 1889; oil on canvas; 18" x 15" (45.7 x 38.1 cm).

057. Robert Henri [1865–1929]; *Girl Seated by the Sea;* 1893; oil on canvas; 18" x 24" (45.7 x 61 cm).

058. Ernest Lawson [1873–1939]; *Spring Night, Harlem River;* 1913; oil on canvas mounted on panel; 25⅛" x 30⅛" (63.8 x 76.5 cm).

059. Maximilien Luce [1858–1941]; *Notre Dame;* 1899; oil on canvas; 32" x 21½" (81.3 x 54.6 cm).

060. Edouard Manet [1832–83]; *Peonies;* 1864; oil on canvas; 36⅝" x 27½" (93 x 70 cm).

061. EDOUARD MANET [1832–83]; *Boating*; 1874; oil on canvas; 38¼" x 51¼" (97.2 x 130.2 cm).
062. EDOUARD MANET [1832–83]; *A Bar at the Folies-Bergère*; 1881–82; oil on canvas;37¾" x 51¼" (96 x 130 cm).
063. EDOUARD MANET [1832–83]; *The Plum*; 1878; oil on canvas;13 ¼" x 19¾" (33.6 x 50.2 cm).
064. EDOUARD MANET [1832–83]; *Jeanne: Spring*; 1881; oil on canvas; 28⅝" x 20" (73 x 51 cm).
065. EDOUARD MANET [1832–83]; *Steamboat, Seascape or Sea View, Calm Weather*; 1864–65; oil on canvas; 29¼" x 36½" (74 x 93 cm).
066. ALFRED MAURER [1868–1932]; *An Arrangement*; 1901; oil on cardboard; 36" x 31⅞" (91.4 x i1 cm).
067. WILLARD LEROY METCALF [1858–1925]; *Gloucester Harbor*; 1895; oil on canvas; 26" x 28¾" (66 x 73 cm).
068. RICHARD MILLER [1875–1943]; *The Toilette*; 1914; oil on canvas; 38" x 46" (96.5 x 116.8 cm).
069. CLAUDE MONET [1840–1926]; *Waterlilies*; 1914; oil on canvas; 78¾" x 78¾" (200 x 200 cm).
070. CLAUDE MONET [1840–1926]; *Rouen Cathedral, Portal and Tour d'Albane, Full Sunlight, Harmony in Blue and Gold*; 1894; oil on canvas; 42" x 28¾" (106.7 x 73 cm).
071. CLAUDE MONET [1840–1926]; *The Artist's Garden at Vétheuil*; 1880; oil on canvas; 59⅞" x 47⅝" (151.5 x 121 cm.
072. CLAUDE MONET [1840–1926]; *The Walk, Lady with a Parasol*; 1875; oil on canvas; 39⅜" x 31⅞" (100 x 81 cm).
073. CLAUDE MONET [1840–1926] *The Highway Bridge at Argenteuil*; 1874; oil on canvas; 23⅝" x 31⅜" (60 x 79.7 cm).
074. CLAUDE MONET [1840–1926]; *Terrace at Sainte-Adresse*; 1867; oil on canvas; 38⅝" x 51⅛" (98.1 x 129.9 cm).
075. CLAUDE MONET [1840–1926]; *Houses of Parliament, London, Sun Breaking through the Fog*; 1904; oil on canvas; 31⅞" x 36¼" (81 x 92 cm).
076. BERTHE MORISOT [1841–95]; *Summer's Day*; 1879; oil on canvas; 18" x 29⅝" (45.7 x 75.2 cm).
077. BERTHE MORISOT [1841–95]; *On the Balcony*; 1871–72; oil on canvas; 23⅝" x 19⅝" (60 x 50 cm).
078. BERTHE MORISOT [1841–95]; *The Cradle*; 1872; oil on canvas; 22" x 18" (56 x 46 cm).
079. BERTHE MORISOT [1841–95]; *At the Ball*; 1875; oil on canvas; 24 ½" x 20½" (62 x 52 cm).
080. CAMILLE PISSARRO [1830–1903]; *Place du Théâtre Français, Rain*; 1898; oil on canvas; 29" x 36" (73.7 x 91 cm).
081. CAMILLE PISSARRO [1830–1903]; *The Shepherdess*; 1881; oil on canvas; 32" x 25¼" (81 x 64.7 cm).
082. CAMILLE PISSARRO [1830–1903]; *The Garden of Les Mathurins at Pontoise*; 1876; oil on canvas; 44⅝" x 65¼" (113.3 x 165.4 cm).
083. CAMILLE PISSARRO [1830–1903]; *The Red Roofs, Corner of a Village, Winter*; 1877; oil on canvas; 21½" x 25¾" (54.5 x 65.6 cm).
084. JEAN-FRANÇOIS RAFFAELLI [1850–1924]; *Boulevard in Paris*; 1888; tempera on cardboard; 19⅞" x 26⅜" (50.5 x 67 cm).
085. EDWARD REDFIELD [1869–1965]; *Lower New York*; 1910; oil on canvas; 38" x 51" (98.5 x 129.5 cm).
086. ROBERT REID [1862–1929]; *Woman with a Vase of Irises*; 1906; oil on canvas; 34" x 26" (86.4 x 66.1 cm).
087. PIERRE-AUGUSTE RENOIR [1841–1919]; *The Luncheon of the Boating Party*; 1881; oil on canvas; 51" x 68" (129.5 x 172.7 cm).
088. PIERRE-AUGUSTE RENOIR [1841–1919]; *Oarsmen at Chatou*; 1879; oil on canvas; 32" x 39½" (81.3 x 100 cm).
089. PIERRE-AUGUSTE RENOIR [1841–1919]; *Vase of Flowers*; 1886; oil on canvas; 39½" x 31" (101 x 79 cm).
090. PIERRE-AUGUSTE RENOIR [1841–1919]; *La Loge*; 1874; oil on canvas; 58⅝" x 45¼" (148.9 x 115 cm).
091. PIERRE-AUGUSTE RENOIR [1841–1919]; *Girls at the Piano*; 1892; oil on canvas; 45½" x 35½" (116 x 90 cm).
092. THEODORE ROBINSON [1852–96]; *The Wedding March*; 1892; oil on canvas; 22⅜" x 26½" (56.7 x 67.3 cm).
093. THEODORE ROBINSON [1852–96]; *Chicago Columbian Exposition*; 1894; oil on canvas; 25" x 30" (63.5 x 76.2 cm).
094. GUY ROSE [1867–1925]; *The Green Parasol*; 1909; oil on canvas; 31" x 19" (78.7 x 48.3 cm).
095. JOHN SINGER SARGENT [1856–1925]; *A Morning Walk*; 1888; oil on canvas; 26⅜" x 19¾" (67 x 50.2 cm).
096. JOHN SINGER SARGENT [1856–1925]; *Paul Helleu Sketching with his Wife*; 1889; oil on canvas; 26" x 32" (66 x 81.5 cm).
097. JOHN SINGER SARGENT [1856–1925]; *The Breakfast Table*; 1884; oil on canvas; 21¾" x 18¼" (55.2 x 46.4 cm).
098. GEORGES-PIERRE SEURAT [1859–91]; *A Sunday Afternoon on the Island of La Grande Jatte*; 1884–86; oil on canvas; 81⅝" x 121¼" (207.5 x 308.1 cm).
099. GEORGES-PIERRE SEURAT [1859–91]; *Bathing at Asnières*; 1883.; oil on canvas; 79" x 118½" (201 x 301 cm).
100. PAUL SIGNAC [1863–1935]; *Boulevard de Clichy, Snow*; 1886; oil on canvas; 19" x 25¾" (48.1 x 65.6 cm).
101. ALFRED SISLEY [1839–99]; *The Bridge at Villeneuve-la-Garenne*; 1872; oil on canvas; 19½" x 25¾" (49.5 x 65.5 cm).
102. ALFRED SISLEY [1839–99]; *The Flood at Port-Marly*; 1876; oil on canvas; 19⅝" x 24" (50 x 61 cm).
103. ANTONÍN SLAVÍCEK [1870–1910]; *Walking in the Park*; 1897; tempera on card; 27⅜" x 20¾" (69.5 x 52.8 cm).
104. ROBERT SPENCER [1879–1931]; *Repairing the Bridge*; 1913; oil on canvas; 30" x 36" (76.2 x 91.4 cm).
105. SIDNEY STARR [1857–1925]; *The City Atlas*; 1888-89; oil on canvas; 24" x 20" (60.9 x 50.6 cm).
106. PHILIP WILSON STEER [1860–1942]; *Summer at Cowes*; 1888; oil on canvas; 20" x 24" (50.9 x 61.2 cm).
107. EDMUND CHARLES TARBELL [1862–1938]; *Three Sisters—A Study in June Sunlight*; 1890; oil on canvas; 35⅛" x 40⅛" (89.2 x 102.2 cm).
108. EDMUND CHARLES TARBELL [1862–1938]; *The Breakfast Room*; 1903; oil on canvas; 25" x 30" (63.5 x 76.2 cm).
109. JAN TOOROP [1858–1928]; *Three Women with Flowers*; 1885–86; oil on canvas; 43¼" x 37⅜" (110 x 95 cm).
110. HENRI DE TOULOUSE-LAUTREC [1864–1901]; *Woman with Gloves (Honorine Platzer)*; 1891; oil on cardboard; 21¼" x 15¾" (54 x 40 cm).
111. HENRI DE TOULOUSE-LAUTREC [1864–1901]; *La Goulue Arriving at the Moulin Rouge with Two Women*; 1892; oil on cardboard; 31¼" x 23¼" (79.4 x 59 cm).
112. HENRI DE TOULOUSE-LAUTREC [1864–1901]; *Rue des Moulins: The Medical Inspection*; 1894; oil on cardboard; 32¼" x 23⅜" (82 x 59.5 cm).
113. HENRI DE TOULOUSE-LAUTREC [1864–1901]; *Ball at the Moulin Rouge*; 1889–90; oil on canvas; 45¼" x 59" (115 x 150 cm).
114. HENRI DE TOULOUSE-LAUTREC [1864–1901]; *The Toilette*; 1889; oil on cardboard; 26⅜" x 21¼" (67 x 54 cm).
115. JOHN TWACHTMAN [1853–1902]; *White Bridge*; 1900; oil on canvas; 30¼" x 25⅛" (76.8 x 63.8 cm).
116. ROBERT VONNOH [1858–1933]; *In Flanders Field—Where Soldiers Sleep and Poppies Grow*; 1890; oil on canvas; 58" x 104" (147.3 x 264.3 cm).
117. EDOUARD VUILLARD [1868–1940]; *Child in a Room*; 1900; oil on cardboard; 17¼" x 22¾" (43.8 x 57.8 cm).
118. J. ALDEN WEIR [1852–1919]; *Against the Window*; 1884; oil on canvas; 36⅛" x 29½" (91.8 x 74.9 cm).
119. J. ALDEN WEIR [1852–1919]; *Willimantic, Connecticut*; 1903; oil on canvas; 20" x 24" (50.8 x 61 cm).
120. THEODORE WENDEL [1859–1932]; *Bridge at Ipswich*; 1905; oil on canvas; 24¼" x 30" (61.5 x 76.2).